S0-AAC-360

A CLASSIC RETELLING

THE Scarlet Letter

by Nathaniel Hawthorne

nextext

Table of Contents

secret. He eventually forgives Hester, but he is terrified to return home to Chillingworth. Hester tells him that he should leave Boston and begin a new life somewhere else.

18: A Flood of Sunshine
Hester convinces Dimmesdale that he should go away with Pearl and her. When he agrees to the plan, he suddenly feels happy. Hester takes off her scarlet letter and throws it on the bank of the brook. Dimmesdale is worried that Pearl will not like him, but Hester thinks that having a father and a real family will make Pearl happy and more like a "normal" child.

19: The Child at the Brook-Side
Pearl does not want to come to Dimmesdale. Hester demands that Pearl come closer, but Pearl starts screaming and points at Hester's chest. She is upset that the scarlet A is missing. Hester pins the letter back on and asks her daughter to go to Dimmesdale. He kisses Pearl, but she washes away the kiss.

20: The Minister in a Maze
In four days, they will board a ship that will go to Bristol, England. Dimmesdale notices that everything seems different, but it is actually he who has changed. Dimmesdale burns the first sermon he had written for Election Day and stays up all night writing a new one.

He tells the crowd that his chest shows a sign
of his sin. He reveals the mark, then collapses. He
asks God's forgiveness. Then Dimmesdale dies.

24: Conclusion ...

Hawthorne gives several ideas about the mark on
Dimmesdale's chest—it may be a wound Dimmesdale
inflicted upon himself, it could be the result of
Chillingworth's medicine, or it could be a symbol
of his suffering spirit. Hawthorne says that the moral
of his story is to be true, to show your worst traits to the
world rather than to hide them.

Hawthorne also explains what happens to the
rest of the characters. Dimmesdale's death left
Chillingworth nothing to live for—he died soon after
Dimmesdale. Pearl inherited a lot of property and was
able to live well the rest of her life. Hester and Pearl
moved to Europe soon after Dimmesdale's death.
Pearl chose to stay there. Several years later, Hester
returned to Boston. When Hester died, she was
buried next to Dimmesdale. The two graves shared
a tombstone engraved with a scarlet letter A.

Background

17th-Century America

In the 1600s, America had thirteen colonies.
These colonies were:

- New England Colonies: *Massachusetts, New Hampshire, Rhode Island, Connecticut*

- Middle Colonies: *New York, New Jersey, Delaware, Pennsylvania*

- Southern Colonies: *Maryland, Virginia, North Carolina, South Carolina, Georgia*

The British controlled the thirteen colonies. The Spanish controlled the land around Florida, and the French controlled everything to the west.

The Thirteen Colonies A mid-1600s map of the colonies.
▼

Early History

A timeline of early America shows how the country was founded and what it looked like at the time the events in *The Scarlet Letter* take place.

1565—Spanish settlers land at St. Augustine in Florida.

1607—Captain John Smith and others land at Jamestown and establish the first English settlement in America.

1638—Anne Hutchinson is banished from New England for her beliefs.

1650—The events of *The Scarlet Letter* take place around this time.

1773—The Boston Tea Party is staged to protest British taxes on colonists.

1776—Colonists declare their independence from Britain.

1850—Nathaniel Hawthorne publishes *The Scarlet Letter.*

1861—The Civil War begins.

Puritanism

Puritans came to America between 1630 and 1640 and settled in the Massachusetts Bay Colony.

Map of Massachusetts This map, circa 1675, shows Salem, Boston, and Plymouth.

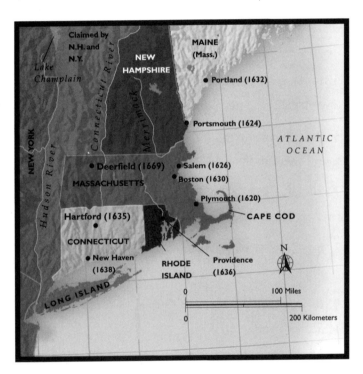

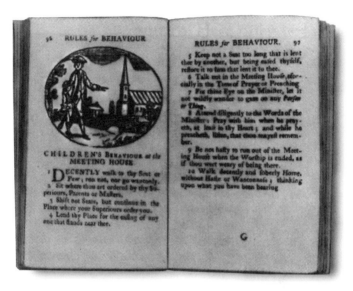

▲

Rules for Behavior This shows strict guidelines children were expected to follow in the classroom.

Puritans

- believed strongly in the Bible

- held the family and work in the highest respect

- took great pride in the way they dressed and how they looked

- governed the land as "God's Elect"

John Winthrop

John Winthrop, the first governor of the
Massachusetts Bay Colony, believed the
Puritans had a special agreement with
God to live together in a moral society.

Life in Early America

The New England Primer A rare copy shows how children learned to read.

▼

Good Children Must

Fear God all day
Parents obey
No false thing say
By no sin stray

Love Christ alway
In secret pray
Mind little play
Make no delay

In doing good.

from *The New England Primer* (1687)

Ducking Stool

When colonists came to America, they brought with them the ducking stool. It was a way to punish people who were accused of gossiping.

The Ducking Stool Officers punish a woman accussed of gossiping.
▼

Family Meal

Puritan families ate meals together. They had napkins but no forks or knives, and all the food was often put in one large pot. Children often had to stand during meals.

Puritan Meal A family gathers for a meal around the table.
▼

Anne Hutchinson

Anne Hutchinson was a religious zealot who was put on trial for what she said and did.

Like Hester Prynne, the main character in *The Scarlet Letter*, Anne Hutchinson "troubled the peace of the commonwealth and churches. . . ." She was expelled from the Massachusetts Bay Colony in 1638.

▲

The Trial An early engraving depicting the trial of Anne Hutchinson.

Puritans of Boston

"Their Laws for Reformation of manners, are very severe, yet but little regarded by the People, so at least as to make 'em better, or cause 'em to mend their manners."

from *Muddy Brains* by John Dunton, March 1686

Nathaniel Hawthorne (1804-1864)

Nathaniel Hawthorne was born in Salem, Massachusetts. His parents came from an important family in Massachusetts Bay Colony. His father was a sea captain, but he died while Hawthorne was just a child.

Hawthorne spent nearly twelve years of his life almost alone, reading and studying about his Puritan ancestors. His stories come from his large knowledge about his Puritan heritage.

Hawthorne published his first stories in 1837. He married in 1842 and settled in Concord, Massachusetts. Hawthorne published *The Scarlet Letter* in 1850. At one point he did work in a customs house, as he describes at the beginning of this novel.

He died in 1864—famous from his writing, but poor, still not able to support himself by his writing.

▲
The Author A photograph of the writer with his work.

The Custom-House

Introductory to "The Scarlet Letter"

When I was younger, I lived in Salem, Massachusetts. I worked in a government building called the Custom-House. All of the items that were brought from out of the state came to the Custom-House first so that taxes could be charged on them. We also kept important documents and records there.

While I worked there, I met many interesting people and heard stories about people who had lived in Salem. From talking to people and reading the records of the town's history, I got ideas for stories that I could write. My job at the Custom-House is what made me become a writer.

One day at the Custom-House, I was searching through some old records for some tax papers. Stuffed in the back of a drawer, I found a bundle of old, yellowed papers. I felt something wrapped inside the papers. When I opened up the tattered paper, a faded piece of cloth fell out. I picked up the piece of cloth. Even though it was old, I could tell that it was once a bright red color. The cloth was in the shape of the letter *A*, and it was decorated with beautiful gold thread.

I had never seen anything like this before, and I wondered what the letter *A* stood for. As I stared at the letter, I noticed that there was writing on the papers that were wrapped around the letter.

Later that night at home, I read the notes that I had found with the cloth *A*. The notes told the story of the scarlet letter and the woman who was forced to wear it. I wanted to know more about the woman, Hester Prynne, and her red letter *A*, so I began to imagine the details and events that were left out of the notes. This is how I came to write the book you are reading now. This is the story of Hester Prynne and her scarlet letter.

CHAPTER ONE

The Prison Door

On a gloomy day, a crowd of angry and curious people in dark **somber**[1] clothing stood outside of a cold-looking building. It was the prison in Boston. The prison was not that old, but its walls were so scarred and rusty that it looked **ancient**.[2] Even the land around the prison was ugly—bare patches of dirt and rough weeds. There was only one thing near the prison that was beautiful—a single, lonesome rosebush.

---

[1] **somber**—gloomy; dull.
[2] **ancient**—very old.

There are many ugly parts to the story I'm going to tell. Maybe, like the little rosebush among the weeds, you'll find something beautiful in this sad **tale**.[3]

---

[3] **tale**—story.

CHAPTER TWO

The Market-Place

Most of the townspeople were gathered across the street from the prison, staring at the prison door. The crowd was **gawking**[1] and grim, waiting for something to happen. In Puritan New England, even the smallest crime caused a **scandal**:[2] the criminal might have to live his or her whole life in shame. The angry crowd was waiting for a well-known criminal to be released from the prison and be punished in front of everyone.

In those days, people had very little understanding for those who didn't follow the law or the strict rules of the church. People who broke laws,

---

[1] **gawking**—staring rudely or stupidly.
[2] **scandal**—a shameful action that makes people shocked.

especially church laws, could be put to death for their crimes. Even small crimes could make a person an **outcast**[3] for his or her entire life.

The women in the crowd were even angrier than the men. Women were taught to be quiet and not give their opinions. But the criminal who was walking out of the prison was a woman. The women of the town were shocked and disgusted by what she had done. A group of five of them was talking about the crime.

"I'll tell you what," said a mean-looking older woman. "I think they should let us women decide the punishment in this case. What do you think? If the five of us picked her punishment, she wouldn't get off so easily."

Another woman said, "I heard that her minister, Reverend Dimmesdale, is very upset that a member of his church would do such a thing."

A third woman spoke, "The judge is a good man, but he was too kind. At the very least, they should have **branded**[4] her forehead. She would have felt that. Instead, she just has to wear a cloth letter on her clothes! That's no punishment! She can cover it up, or she can even decorate it and wear it with pride!"

---

[3] **outcast**—someone who is put away from home or from friends.

[4] **branded**—marked by burning the skin with a hot iron.

A young mother said, "It doesn't matter how she wears the letter. The shame of the letter and what she did will always hurt her."

But the meanest woman of them all said, "Why are we talking about her letter, or branding her forehead? The Bible and the law say that **adultery**[5] should be punished by death. I want to see her hang!"

Suddenly the prison door was opened. The jailer put a hand on the prisoner's shoulder to lead her out, but the woman prisoner pushed the jailer's hand away and stepped bravely out on her own. The proud, serious woman was holding a three month-old baby to her chest. She clutched the baby tightly to protect her from the light . . . and to hide the red letter *A* sewn to the front of her shirt. Then she lowered the baby, and everyone could see the red letter.

What they saw shocked them. Everyone **gasped**[6] at the red *A* and the fancy stitching and flashy gold thread that the woman had used to decorate the letter.

---

[5] **adultery**—sex between someone who is married and someone who is not his or her husband or wife.

[6] **gasped**—breathed as if surprised.

The young woman standing before the crowd was tall and attractive. She had a confident and **determined**[7] look in her eyes. The townspeople who had known Hester Prynne before she was **disgraced**,[8] before she entered the prison, expected her to come out a changed woman. They thought that she would be ashamed and sorry, that she would lose her bright and confident attitude. But few of the people in the crowd even noticed Hester. Instead, everyone stared at the scarlet letter—the bright, bold, red cloth *A*. It was decorated with the fanciest needlework and designs that anyone had ever seen.

The five women who had been **gossiping**[9] about Hester were shocked by the bold decorations that Hester had added to the letter. She was supposed to have been embarrassed by the punishment.

"She is very talented at sewing," said one. "But look at how she shows off her talents. She should be ashamed!"

Another said, "I'd like to tear that flashy dress off her. Instead she should wear filthy rags."

The youngest of the group, the one who had tried to show some sympathy earlier, said, "Enough,

---

[7] **determined**—with someone's mind fully made up.

[8] **disgraced**—lost the respect and approval of others.

[9] **gossiping**—talking about other people and their private business. (Gossip is not always the truth.)

all of you! You can be sure that every stitch she put on that letter stabbed her right in her heart."

The jailer had to push the crowd back as he led Hester away from the jail. He said, "Clear a path! I will take the prisoner where every man, woman, and child can see her. As part of her punishment, she must stand for three hours on the **scaffold**[10] in the marketplace at the center of town. Then everyone can see how we treat people who break God's Laws."

> **"You can be sure that every stitch she put on that letter stabbed her right in her heart."**

It was only a short trip from the prison to the marketplace. But, to Hester, the walk seemed as if it would never end. She and the guard were at the front of a **pitiful**[11] parade. The whole way to the scaffold, **grim**[12]-faced men, **mean-spirited**[13] women, and curious children followed Hester. At last, she reached the platform, which stood facing the busiest part of town. It was directly in front of the area's oldest and largest church.

---

[10] **scaffold**—a platform or stage.

[11] **pitiful**—deserving scorn.

[12] **grim**—without mercy; harsh.

[13] **mean-spirited**—very unkind; narrow-minded.

Without even **hesitating**,[14] Hester climbed the stairs and stood bravely in front of the growing crowd. The platform she stood on was about shoulder height—everyone in town could see her and stare at her. No one in the crowd laughed or teased Hester. Each person watching imagined how **mortified**[15] they would be if they had to face Hester's punishment. To some people, Hester's punishment might not seem that awful. But at that time, being put to death was the only thing worse than being **humiliated**[16] in front of everyone. To make things worse for Hester, many important people—even the governor—were sitting on another platform above her. The men looked down on her from their seats.

Hester was ready for people's insults. What she wasn't ready for was the pain of having five hundred angry neighbors and former friends staring gravely at her. For three hours! There were moments when Hester felt that she would go crazy, that she would scream to break the tension and the silence. But then there were moments when the crowd below her seemed to **vanish**[17] completely. As she was staring at the angry, disapproving faces, the crowd

---

[14] **hesitating**—stopping or pausing.
[15] **mortified**—ashamed.
[16] **humiliated**—made to feel ashamed.
[17] **vanish**—disappear.

would fade away, and she would think about more pleasant things.

Hester thought of some happy times in her past. She thought about her childhood home in England, far away from this place. She could see her parents, friends, and favorite places. In her imagination, she saw another face—the thin, pale face of an older man. She also remembered the house and life that she and this man were supposed to share. Suddenly, her memories vanished. She found herself on the scaffold again, with the whole town staring at her.

She looked down at the scarlet *A* with shock and sadness. She felt as though none of this could be happening. She hugged the baby tightly to her chest in shock, causing the baby to cry out. Hester looked down and touched the letter, then the baby, to remind herself that her baby and her shame were real. Yes, these were real, and everything else in her life no longer mattered.

CHAPTER THREE

The Recognition

As she stared out at the crowd, Hester suddenly noticed a man at the edge of the crowd—a man she recognized. He was a small, hump-backed man with a thin, pale face. He was standing next to an Indian, and he looked strange and **shabby**[1] in his mixture of Indian and Puritan clothes. As soon as Hester saw the man, she clutched the baby to her chest, causing the baby to cry out again.

When the thin, pale man had first arrived at the edge of the crowd, he hadn't even noticed Hester. But now he was staring right at her. A look of shock passed across his face. As he stared at Hester, she began to stare back. When he realized that Hester

---

[1] **shabby**—worn and faded.

knew who he was, he raised a single finger to his lips. His actions told Hester to keep quiet.

The shabby, bent man turned to another man in the crowd and asked, "Excuse me, sir, but who is this woman? Why is she being punished like this?"

"You must be new in town if you don't know Hester Prynne," said the man.

"You're right," said the stranger. "I have been gone for many years, and I had bad luck on land and on the sea. The Indians held me as their prisoner. Please—tell me about this Hester Prynne. What has she done to deserve such a terrible punishment?"

"I'll tell you. After all the bad luck you've had, you'll be glad to learn that you are in a God-fearing town where people obey laws. When people break the law—like this woman did—we catch them and punish them. This woman, Hester Prynne, was married to an educated Englishman. They lived in Holland for a while and planned to move to America. The Englishman sent his wife to America first. She was to set up their house while the **scholar**[2] finished his business in Holland. Master Prynne, the English scholar, has not been heard from in two years. No one here or in Holland knows

---

[2] **scholar**—a person having much knowledge.

what happened to him. His wife, a beautiful young woman—that woman up on the scaffold—was left alone for two years. In the end, she gave into her **temptation**.[3] You can see, by the three-month-old baby in her arms, that the father of the child couldn't have been Hester's husband. He has been missing for two years! Everyone knows that she has broken the law and committed a serious sin. She slept with another man while who knows what has happened to her husband."

> *"Everyone knows that she has broken the law and committed a serious sin."*

The stoop-shouldered little man's eyes were angry, but he had a bitter smile on his face.

"So, tell me, who is this baby's father?"

"No one knows," said the other man. "She refuses to tell, no matter what punishment she is threatened with. The guilty man may even be right here in this crowd, trying to hide what he has done. He forgets that God can see him, even if we can't."

The stranger said, "Maybe the husband should come back and try to solve this mystery. He could

---

[3] **temptation**—something that tries to make a person do something wrong, usually just for the person's pleasure.

make his wife talk. At least he could have **revenge**[4] on the man who did this to his wife."

"He probably could make her talk," said the other man. "But he could be at the bottom of the ocean somewhere. Maybe he is a prisoner of the Indians, like you were. The judges have been **merciful**[5] with her. Usually, the punishment for adultery is death. Since Hester is so young, and because her husband has been missing so long, the judges have given her this light **sentence**.[6] She only has to stand before the crowd for three hours. Then she has to wear that red *A*, which stands for *Adultery*, on all of her clothes for the rest of her life."

"That's a wise sentence," said the thin, pale man. "She will be a living warning to anyone who might be tempted by sin. What makes me furious, though, is that the man who sinned with her isn't up there to be punished too. He may think he's going to get away with what he did to that man's wife, but he will be known! Believe me, he will be known! He will be known!" After saying that, the man turned to his Indian friend, whispered a few words, and left.

---

[4] **revenge**—an act of punishment in order to get even.

[5] **merciful**—mild, kind; not severe.

[6] **sentence**—a decision a judge makes to punish a criminal.

While the villager and the stranger were talking, Hester had stared only at the stranger. She was staring so hard at him, she felt like no one else was there—just her and the man. Hester wondered what it would have been like if she had been alone when she had run into this man. When she thought about speaking to him face-to-face, she was glad that the crowd was around her.

Hester was startled when a strong voice from above boomed out, "Hester Prynne, listen to me!" Hester turned to the **balcony**[7] above and behind her. The governor, the highest church officials, and other important men sat there. The booming voice belonged to the Reverend John Wilson, the most powerful man in the Massachusetts Church.

"Hester Prynne, I have met with your minister, Reverend Dimmesdale," he said, putting his hand on the shoulder of the young minister next to him. "I told him that he should deal with you and your awful sin, right here in front of everyone. Because he knows you better than I do, I thought he might persuade you to reveal your partner in evil, the father of your baby. But the Reverend Dimmesdale here thinks it's wrong to force a woman to reveal her secrets in the town square in front of all her

---

[7] **balcony**—outside platform built off the side of a building and enclosed by a railing.

neighbors. I think that the woman in this case has already sinned, and her sin, the baby, can be seen by everyone."

Then the governor challenged Dimmesdale in front of everyone. "Dimmesdale, you are responsible for saving this woman's soul. How are you going to make her tell her secret?"

Everyone's eyes then turned to Dimmesdale. He was a well-educated young minister, fresh from the finest schools in England. Dimmesdale was well-known in the town—he was smart, **enthusiastic**,[8] and gave excellent sermons. People thought very highly of Dimmesdale, but lately he had seemed nervous in public and had begun to spend more and more time alone.

The governor spoke again, "Speak to the woman, brother Dimmesdale. Remember, her soul is in your hands. Because you are responsible for her soul, your soul is at risk, too."

Reverend Dimmesdale bent his head, either to say a prayer or to collect his thoughts. He stood up and spoke to Hester.

"Hester Prynne, you must tell us who shares your guilt. If you feel it would ease your mind and

---

[8] **enthusiastic**—eagerly interested.

save your soul, you must name the man. Even if he has a high and respected position in our town, and your naming him would ruin him for life, it would be better for you to tell who he is. Otherwise, he will have to live his whole life in secret guilt. Whoever he is, he'll have to treat you like you're guilty when he sees you in public. If you don't identify him, you'll force him to add **hypocrisy**[9] to his sin. After all, he'll have to treat you with disgust and disapproval, all the while knowing that he is just as guilty as you are. Please, Hester, do the man a favor. Tell the whole town who he is."

The young minister had a rich, sweet, powerful voice that would have persuaded almost anyone in the crowd. Even Hester's baby seemed strangely attracted to him—she broke into a smile and stretched out her arms when Dimmesdale spoke. Dimmesdale's speech was so powerful that everyone in the crowd was sure Hester would either name her partner or the guilty man would step forward and admit his sin.

Reverend Wilson's voice boomed out, "Speak, woman. Only if you **confess**[10] and ask forgiveness can the letter be removed from your chest."

---

[9] **hypocrisy**—only pretending to be very good or religious.

[10] **confess**—admit what one has done wrong.

Then more voices rang out from the crowd. "Speak!" "Tell us!" "Tell us the man's name, and give your daughter a father!"

"I will not speak," said Hester. "My daughter must find a father in Heaven, because she'll never have a father here."

"She will not speak," whispered Dimmesdale, wiping the sweat from his forehead. "She is strong and generous . . . she will not speak."

The Reverend Wilson stood up, ready to try his best to persuade Hester. He spoke for over an hour, spending most of his time telling about Hester's sin and the red letter she wore. Hester stood in front of the crowd, seeming to pay no attention to the long and powerful sermon. Toward the end of the sermon, the baby began to scream and cry. Hester tried to comfort and quiet the baby, but her thoughts were far away.

At the end of the long three hours, Hester was led down from the scaffold. As she walked away from the crowd and back into the dark mouth of the jail door, the calm, strong look on her face did not change.

CHAPTER FOUR

The Interview

Once she was back in her cell, Hester became nervous. She seemed so tense and upset that the jailer was afraid that she might hurt herself or the baby. The baby, Pearl, was sick too. She was curled up and crying out in pain. When he couldn't calm Hester or help the baby, the jailer sent for a doctor. The jailer told Hester to stop worrying. The doctor was a good doctor, trained in the finest schools in England.

When the jailer returned to Hester's cell, the **hunchbacked**[1] man—the one Hester had seen in the crowd—was following him.

---

[1] **hunchbacked**—having a backbone that curves out, forming a hump.

"This is Roger Chillingworth," said the jailer, who noticed the surprised look on Hester's face.

"Leave me with my patient," said Chillingworth. "Both she and the baby will feel calmer soon." Chillingworth then mixed herbs into a **potion**[2] and turned to Hester.

"Here, woman, give this to your child. She won't recognize my face or voice as someone she can trust, so she may not take it from me. You give it to her."

Hester pushed the medicine away from the baby and said, "I can't believe you'd take your revenge out on an innocent child."

"I have no problems with this child," said Chillingworth, "only with how she was created. The medicine is safe. If this were my own child, I would give her this medicine."

When Hester **hesitated**,[3] he picked up the medicine and gave it to Pearl himself. Pearl quieted down and quickly fell asleep.

"I also have a potion to help you relax, Hester." Hester held the cup up to her lips.

"I've thought about killing myself," she said. "Do you plan on killing me with this potion? If you do, think about how guilty you would feel. I really am going to drink this now."

---

[2] **potion**—a drink used for medicine or for magic.
[3] **hesitated**—to hold back due to uncertainty.

"Go ahead and drink it," the man said. "Don't you know me better than that? Besides, if I wanted to punish you for what you've done to me, I'd let you live forever with your **humiliation**[4] and shame. Drink the medicine and go on living. In the eyes of your neighbors, and in my eyes—the eyes of the man you once called husband—you will live in shame."

> *"In the eyes of your neighbors, and in my eyes—the eyes of the man you once called husband—you will live in shame."*

Hester sighed and took the medicine. Then she sat down next to her husband. She had thought that she would never see him again.

Chillingworth spoke, "Hester, I'm not going to ask what happened, or what caused you to be **unfaithful**[5] to me. What you did is not right, but I understand why you were tempted. How could I have expected someone as young and beautiful as you to find happiness with someone like me? I understand now that you never loved me. And I know that you never will love me. I paid more attention to my books than I did to you. I should have known that this would happen. I can't blame you."

---

[4] **humiliation**—a lowering of pride or self-respect.
[5] **unfaithful**—not true to the vows of marriage.

"I have wronged you, but I never lied to you," said Hester. "You knew I didn't love you."

"I know," said Chillingworth, "but I couldn't give up on my dream of a happy, normal life. My heart was a cold, dark house, longing for warmth. I spent my life studying—alone and serious. But I always wanted someone to love. So I thought I could make you happy, make you love me. But I was doomed to a cold and lonely life. And I should have known that a woman like you couldn't live a life like that. So, I have done wrong to you, and now you have done wrong to me. I'd say the scale is balanced[6] evenly between you and me. I want no revenge against you, but I will have my revenge against the man who wronged me! Who is he, so that I can deliver my punishment to him?"

> **"The scale is balanced . . . I want no revenge against you, but I will have my revenge against the man who wronged me!"**

"Don't ask me," Hester said firmly, "because I'll never tell you."

"I'll never know him? Hester, there is almost no fact that can be hidden from me—my job is to

---

[6] the scale is balanced—both Hester and Chillingworth have had something wrong done to them, and they have both done something wrong. They "are even."

find facts! You can hide the man from the minister and from the judges, but I will look everywhere for him. I will always be looking for him. Someday, when he and I pass each other, he will **shudder,**[7] and I will feel a chill. Then we will both know that the hunt is over."

All this time, Chillingworth's soft and mild features were dark with anger, and his eyes glowed like flaming coals. Hester was almost **spellbound**[8] by his speech—she covered her heart with her hands, because she was afraid that Chillingworth could read the man's name there.

"I will find him, Hester. I won't try to take God's place by taking away his life. Nor will I bring him to judgment in a court of law. But I will find him and make him suffer for the rest of his life, just like you and I will always suffer. You've sworn to keep his secret. Let me warn you: you must also keep mine! No one here knows who I am. Make sure it stays that way. Don't **betray**[9] me!"

"Why not?" asked Hester. "Why don't you tell the world who you are and **disown**[10] me?"

"Maybe because I don't want the shame and embarrassment of everyone knowing that my wife

---

[7] **shudder**—shake with horror or cold.

[8] **spellbound**—too interested to move.

[9] **betray**—tell a secret to someone.

[10] **disown**—cast off; give up.

is unfaithful. Maybe I have other reasons for keeping who I am a secret. Just don't tell anyone my secret, especially the father of your child. His reputation—and his life—will be in my hands!"

"I'll tell no one, I swear it," said Hester. And for the first time that long day, she felt truly afraid.

Suddenly, Chillingworth acted as if he were just the doctor, a man whom the prisoner did not know.

"Well, Hester Prynne, I hope that the medicine makes you and the child feel better." Then a cold, almost cruel smile crossed his face. "I'll leave you alone with your letter and your shame. I wonder if that letter will burn into your body and fill your sleep with nightmares."

Hester was troubled by the evil look in his eyes. "Why are you looking at me like that? Have you become a servant of the Devil? By asking me to keep your secret, have you tricked me into some deal that will ruin my soul?"

"Not your soul," said Chillingworth with another chilling smile. "Your soul is not in danger."

CHAPTER FIVE

Hester at Her Needle

Hester was released from jail. The sun shone brightly on the bright red letter *A* and the fancy gold thread.

The judges told her that she could go anywhere she wanted—to England, back to Holland, or anywhere in the **colonies**.[1] Instead, she chose to stay in Boston, where everyone knew of her crime and her shame. Instead of running away, she and Pearl lived in a little **cottage**[2] just outside of town, by the sea. Hester stayed at the site of the worst event of her life, like a ghost haunting the scene of some

---

[1] **colonies**—land settled by people who left England and came to live in America.

[2] **cottage**—small house.

tragedy.[3] Deep down, Hester realized that part of the reason she stayed was to be near the father of her baby. She knew that they could never be together—she was married, and he had a high place in the community. Still, she hoped to be with him after they both died.

Hester lived away from the rest of town, but she saw townspeople every day. She supported herself by doing sewing for the women of the town. She was the most skilled **seamstress**[4] in all of Boston. The clothes Hester sewed were very popular. Although the Puritans generally dressed in simple, somber clothes, her fancy **embroidery**[5] was in demand for clothes for all ceremonies and special occasions. Because of the crime she had committed, however, she was not allowed to create wedding dresses. No bride would wear a dress created by someone who had committed adultery.

But even though the women admired her work, they abused Hester and treated her like the lowest criminal. The men glared at her or ignored her. They were afraid to speak to her. No man wanted

---

[3] **tragedy**—a very sad or terrible happening.

[4] **seamstress**—a woman whose work is sewing.

[5] **embroidery**—decorative sewing or stitching.

anyone to think that he was the secret lover who was too **cowardly**[6] to confess. Most children did not know about Hester's crime. They did know that she was different, and they were afraid of her.

Even though everyone hated and mistreated her, Hester was patient. People were cold to her and abused her, but she didn't fight back. Many times Hester even thought of praying for the people who treated her so badly, but she was afraid to. Hester thought that even her prayers would turn into curses.

This is the way that Hester lived— punished by others and punishing herself.

Even though she loved fancy clothes, Hester wore plain, ugly dresses, decorated only by the bright red *A*. Her daughter, Pearl, however, wore the most colorful and attractive outfits anyone had ever seen. Pearl's bright, unusual clothes matched her personality. Pearl was a bright, happy, and **mischievous**[7] child, full of energy and spirit. She was so free-spirited and strong-willed that she was hard to control.

Not only did Hester sew for the people in town, she also helped those who were in need.

---

[6] **cowardly**—running from danger or trouble.
[7] **mischievous**—naughty.

Even though she tried hard to be helpful, the towns-people still looked down on Hester. This is the way that Hester lived—punished by others and punishing herself.

CHAPTER SIX

Pearl

The name Hester gave her daughter, "Pearl," is a name that many people think shows calm, peace, and **purity**.[1] But this is not why Hester chose the name. She chose it because of a Bible passage about a single pearl, bought at a high price. That is just how Hester got Pearl. She had paid a high price, and Pearl was her only treasure. Hester loved her child, but she didn't know if a good child could come from her evil act of passion with her secret lover.

Pearl was a beautiful, bright girl. Her mother used all of her skill to create for her daughter the most beautiful clothes. Pearl did not always obey her mother and did not respond to any kind of

---

[1] **purity**—cleanness; freedom from evil.

punishment. No matter what Hester tried, Pearl followed her own wishes and did only what she wanted to do.

During Pearl's first three years, Pearl and Hester spent all of their time together. When the two went on walks, other children would sometimes walk up to Pearl and try to play with her. Pearl wanted nothing to do with the Puritan children—they teased her, and they treated her mother badly. Whenever the Puritan children were near, Pearl would throw stones and shout at them to get back at them for the way they treated her and her mother. Pearl had a rich imagination. When she was alone, the trees, flowers—even a bunch of rags—became her playmates. But often, instead of treating these imaginary playmates as friends, she fought with them as if they were enemies.

Because she lived alone with her mother and never had any contact with anyone else, Pearl was a strange child in many ways. She had always been fascinated by the scarlet letter. When she was a tiny baby, the first thing that Pearl had noticed was the scarlet letter. One summer afternoon, Pearl picked up handfuls of wild flowers and threw them at the letter, one by one. At first, Hester tried to cover the letter. But then she thought that maybe this was part of her punishment. Hester simply stood and looked sadly at her little girl, while Pearl kept throwing the flowers.

One time, when Hester was looking into Pearl's eyes, she imagined seeing a demon looking back at her. What she imagined scared her. When Hester tried to discuss religion with Pearl (since they were unwelcome in the churches), Pearl would **deny**[2] that she had a "Heavenly Father." Hester would tell Pearl that she was a gift from God. Pearl would just laugh and ask, "Where did I come from?"

---

[2] **deny**—say that something is not true; to not accept.

CHAPTER SEVEN

The Governor's Hall

One day, Hester went to the Governor's mansion to deliver a pair of gloves that he had ordered. Hester had decorated the gloves with her finest stitching[1] so the Governor could wear them for special occasions. But delivering the gloves was not the only reason for her visit.

More and more often, Hester had overheard people in town saying that Pearl should be taken away from her. People said that, because Pearl was the result of a sinful affair, Pearl was evil. People believed that Hester would never be able to turn her life around if she were raising and living with a servant of the devil. Others said that Hester was

---

[1] **stitching**—needlework, embroidery.

the evil one, and that Pearl should be taken away and raised by someone with better morals than Hester. Hester needed to convince the Governor to let her keep her own child.

For this special meeting with the Governor, Hester made a new dress for Pearl to wear. It was scarlet red, cut very narrow at the top with a wide, full skirt. Not only was this dress shaped like Hester's A, but it was also covered with the same fancy, gold stitching.

Some people who saw the dress thought that Hester was making fun of her punishment. Others thought that Hester was just showing that she would not let the punishment destroy her—she was showing the world that she would not try to hide from what she had done.

As Hester and Pearl walked to the Governor's house, they met a group of Puritan children about Pearl's age. The children grabbed rocks and **clods**[2] of mud and dirt and got ready to throw them at Hester and Pearl. Just one minute before, Pearl had been running alongside her mother, carefree and lighthearted. But as soon as she was threatened by the other children, she stomped her feet, shook her fists, and began yelling and screaming to protect herself and her mother. This bold attack frightened

---

[2] **clods**—lumps.

the children and sent them running off for a safe place to hide. Once the children were gone, Pearl returned to her earlier, happier mood.

When they reached the Governor's mansion, the doorman told them that the Governor was very busy with two ministers and a doctor of some sort. The doorman told them they could wait inside until the Governor was ready to see them.

As the mother and daughter wandered the main hall, they came across the Governor's own suit of **armor**.[3] Pearl was fascinated by the armor and how bright and shiny it was.

She stared at it for several minutes before yelling, "Mother, come look! Look here, I can see you on the armor." The armor was so highly polished that Pearl and Hester could clearly see Hester's **image**[4] reflected on the curved chest of the armor suit. But because of where Hester was standing and because of the outward curve of the chest piece, Hester's image was oddly **distorted**.[5] The red A was enlarged many times—it looked to be almost as large as Hester herself. Hester pulled Pearl away from the armor and sat her by a window that looked out onto the garden.

---

[3] **armor**—metal protective covering used in battle.

[4] **image**—a likeness or copy.

[5] **distorted**—twisted out of shape.

"Let's look at the flowers in this garden," said Hester. "I'm sure they are more beautiful than any flowers we see in the woods." Pearl especially liked the rich red roses just outside the window. She began to cry loudly, begging for one of the roses. Hester tried to hush Pearl, but everything she did to calm her made her cry more loudly.

Soon, Hester heard voices in the garden. When the door **latch**[6] clicked, Pearl stopped crying and looked to see who would come through the door.

---

[6] **latch**—hook for fastening or closing a door or gate.

CHAPTER EIGHT

The Elf-Child and the Minister

Governor Bellingham and the Reverend John Wilson, the leader of the Boston church, were the first men to come through the door. Behind them came Reverend Dimmesdale and Roger Chillingworth. In the three years or so since Chillingworth had come to town, he had earned a reputation as a skilled doctor. He was Reverend Dimmesdale's personal doctor and had become his close friend as well. Dimmesdale needed a doctor of his own, because his health seemed to get worse each week. He always looked sickly, nervous, and exhausted. Most people in town thought that Dimmesdale's poor health was caused by his hard work. As a minister, the needs of his church were very demanding. Chillingworth, however, began to wonder if something else—something secret—was wearing away at Dimmesdale.

When the Governor stepped into the hall, Pearl was standing right in front of him.

"What are you? Are you some elf or a small ghost sent to haunt my house?" he asked jokingly. "Are you a Christian child? Do you know your prayers and study the Bible?"

When the Governor and his guests looked past Pearl, they saw Hester standing behind her. Then they realized who Pearl was.

"Oh," said the Governor, "you are just the child we were talking about. You have come at a good time. We are trying to decide what should be done with you."

"Hester Prynne," said the Governor, "tell me why we shouldn't take this child away from you. She should be raised by a good, Christian mother who can **discipline**[1] her and teach her morals. What values can you teach this girl?"

Hester replied bravely, "I can teach her the things that this has taught me!" While saying this,

---

[1] **discipline**—punish or train through instruction.

Hester pointed to the scarlet letter on her chest. "I learn from it every day. If I can teach its lessons to my daughter, she will be saved from my fate, even though I can't be."

The Reverend Wilson sat down and called Pearl to him. "Let's see if your mother has raised you as a good Christian," he said. "Little Pearl, who made you?"

Pearl had been taught religion by her mother, and she knew the answer that the reverend expected to hear. But she refused to answer the question.

Finally, she said, "No one made me. I am a rose that was picked off the rosebush that grows outside the prison door!"

Chillingworth smiled, then whispered something to Reverend Dimmesdale. Hester noticed how much Chillingworth had changed in the last few years. He looked darker, more evil, and more physically **deformed**[2] than he did before.

Reverend Wilson stood up. "Hester Prynne," he said, "your daughter can't even tell me who created her. It's clear that you aren't giving her a proper Christian upbringing. I've made up my mind. She will be taken away from you."

---

[2] **deformed**—disfigured; made into the wrong shape.

Hester grabbed Pearl and then stepped angrily toward the old minister.

"God gave me Pearl, to be my reward for all that I have lost. He also gave her to me as my punishment. Every time I see her, I think of my sin. Look—she has become a living scarlet letter. Although she represents my sin, she is God's way of helping me learn right from wrong. You cannot take her!"

Hester then turned to Reverend Dimmesdale. "Speak up for me! You were my pastor[3] and responsible for my soul. You know me better than they do. Speak up for me and my right to keep my child."

Dimmesdale stepped forward, looking more sickly and weak than ever. "She is right. God has made this mother and this strange child to be together. Who else knows how to handle this odd little girl? I think the girl is good for the mother, too. God gave her the child as a curse, to remind her of her shame every day. He also gave her the child as a blessing, to teach Hester to accept

> *"God gave me Pearl, to be my reward for all that I have lost. He also gave her to me as my punishment."*

---

[3] **pastor**—minister; someone who is in charge of a church.

her wrong and to learn to love as God wants her to. The child is God's way of sharing love and forgiveness, even for this sinner." Dimmesdale went on and on, giving a moving **sermon**,[4] though only a few were there to hear it.

Then Chillingworth spoke. "You seem to take an unusual interest in this case, my friend."

The Governor slapped Dimmesdale on the shoulder, nearly knocking him over. "You have **persuaded**[5] me, young minister. The child will remain with her mother, but she must receive weekly religious education from you."

Exhausted after his speech, Dimmesdale walked away from the group. Pearl also slipped away and snuck over to Dimmesdale. She took his hand and rubbed it against her cheek. Hester had never seen such a sweet and tender act from her little child. Dimmesdale took Pearl's head in his hands. He looked around, hesitating for a moment. Then, quickly, he gave Pearl a kiss on the forehead and turned away.

Chillingworth watched the little girl as she skipped happily down the hall.

"She sure has a lot of her mother in her," he said. "I wonder, Governor, if some wise man could

---

[4] **sermon**—public talk about religion, usually part of a church service.

[5] **persuaded**—causing someone to do or believe something.

study her personality in order to figure out who her father really is."

As Pearl and Hester left the Governor's house, Mistress Hibbins, the Governor's sister, was entering. Hibbins (who, a few years later, would be put to death for being a witch) pulled Hester aside.

"Come join us deep in the forest tonight," she said. "We are holding a ceremony to bring the Black Man[6] to us, and I have promised him that you will join our dark party."

"Tell Satan that I have to stay home with my little girl," Hester smiled **triumphantly**.[7] "But if they had taken her from me, I would have come. I would have been glad to sign my name in the Black Man's book."

"You'll join us someday," Hibbins said, walking away.

This meeting between Hester and Mistress Hibbins proved that Dimmesdale was right—Pearl did keep Hester on the "straight and narrow path." If Pearl had been taken from her, Hester probably would have gone to the forest that night to meet with the Devil.

---

[6] Black Man—the Devil.

[7] **triumphantly**—with the feeling that one has won.

CHAPTER NINE

The Leech[1]

None of the townspeople, not even Dimmesdale, had figured out that "Roger Chillingworth" was actually Hester's long-lost husband. Not wanting to be associated with Hester's shame, he continued to keep his identity a secret. In fact, for a while, Chillingworth was very popular in town. Having learned about medicine in his studies, he was easily able to trick the townspeople into believing he was a real doctor. Many people believed he was a gift to the town from God, sent to heal and care for Reverend Dimmesdale. Although the young reverend seemed to grow paler and more sickly

[1] leech—old term for doctor. The term refers to the practice of placing leeches (a kind of worm) on patients in order to suck out some of the patient's blood. Doctors at the time believed that evil in the blood caused sickness.

each day, Dimmesdale had said that he needed no medicine or doctor's treatment, until he accepted Chillingworth's care.

The two men began to spend more and more time together. As their friendship grew, Chillingworth convinced Dimmesdale that they should live in the same house. Although they had separate rooms, the doctor was able to keep a close eye on his patient.

They thought that the devil and God were fighting over Reverend Dimmesdale's soul . . . and they wondered who would win.

Although the reverend's friends were pleased that the doctor was taking such a strong interest in Dimmesdale's health, some people in the town thought the old doctor was up to something. Soon, the people in town began to notice that Chillingworth was getting uglier and acting stranger. Some of the townspeople began to doubt that he was really a doctor. They began to suspect that Chillingworth practiced "Black Magic." As Chillingworth's looks and attitude changed, some people came to believe that the doctor was either the Devil himself or one of his helpers. They thought that the Devil and God were fighting over Reverend Dimmesdale's soul . . . and they wondered who would win.

CHAPTER TEN

The Leech and His Patient

Throughout his life, Chillingworth had been a kind and decent man. When he began his "investigation" to learn if Dimmesdale had been Hester's lover, Chillingworth was at first calm and neutral. But, as Chillingworth began to pry the secret from Dimmesdale, he became more **obsessed**.[1]

As time went on, Chillingworth became cruel. He played tricks to make Dimmesdale confess. His obsession with finding Hester's lover took over his mind, his life, and his soul. He would not stop searching until he found the truth.

---

[1] **obsessed**—focused on only one thing.

One day, Dimmesdale was especially tired, nervous, and weary. Chillingworth knew that Dimmesdale was at a weak point in his life, so he chose this time to try to trick him into confessing.

Chillingworth said to Dimmesdale, "Dimmesdale, old friend, in your experience as a minister, have you been able to figure out why some men refuse to confess their secret sins? After all, everyone knows that keeping dark secrets is dangerous for the body and the soul."

His obsession with finding Hester's lover took over his mind, his life, and his soul.

Dimmesdale replied, "Most men do confess their sins and find peace of body and mind. But some men are not able to confess. They may need to keep secrets because they have positions in the community that they don't want to lose. If men like this went public with their secrets, they would be declared sinful. They wouldn't be permitted to go on doing God's work."

"Oh, Dimmesdale, I disagree. Don't you think that God would be better served if the guilty man told the truth, confessed his sin, and were forgiven?"

At this, Dimmesdale turned away and quickly changed the subject. A broad, **gleeful**[2] smile crossed Chillingworth's face. He felt he was getting closer to breaking Dimmesdale and making him tell his secret. Just as Dimmesdale walked away from Chillingworth, he noticed Hester and Pearl crossing by the cemetery next door. His attention was caught by Pearl's mischievous, playful mood. She skipped across graves and headstones, and she had decorated her mother's red *A* with burrs from a weed.

Chillingworth joined Dimmesdale at the window, and the two discussed Pearl's strange behavior.

Chillingworth wondered aloud, "What kind of child is this? Does she even know right from wrong?" Pearl heard the men's voices and looked up at the window. A naughty smile lit up Pearl's face, and then she ran away from the window.

"Get away from the Devil in the window, Mother," she shouted, laughing. "Get away or he'll catch you. He already caught the Reverend Dimmesdale!" This last comment sent a chill through Dimmesdale as he turned away from the window.

Chillingworth put his arm around his friend. "Dimmesdale," he said, "your health is getting worse. I feel you shivering. Do you have a fever?"

---

[2] **gleeful**—very happy; joyous.

"No, no, it's not that," Dimmesdale mumbled.

"You know," Chillingworth said, "I believe that the mind and the body are connected. An illness of one causes an illness of the other. Tell me what troubles you. Maybe I can figure out what the problem is, if you'll let me look inside your heart. I can never cure you as long as you hide anything from me."

> *"The only one who can cure me is the Physician of the soul."*

"I know what my illness is," Dimmesdale said. "I don't have an illness of the body. Mine is a sickness of the soul. I'm glad you want to help cure me, but I'll never reveal my secrets to any doctor here on earth. The only one who can cure me is the Physician of the soul.[3] I have told all my secrets to Him. Who are you to try to **meddle**[4] in my relationship with God!"

Dimmesdale was so upset by this discussion that he bolted from the room.

"This is the kind of man he is," said Chillingworth to himself, "the kind of man who lets his emotions run away with him, who gets upset and makes mistakes. The Reverend Arthur Dimmesdale

---

[3] Physician of the soul—God.

[4] **meddle**—interfere in someone else's business.

has let his passion cause him to make mistakes before," he laughed.

It didn't take long for Dimmesdale and Chillingworth to become friends again. Dimmesdale felt bad that he had spoken so rudely to the doctor, and he apologized sincerely. One day, while they were reading in the same room, Dimmesdale fell into a deep sleep. When Chillingworth was sure that Dimmesdale was fast sleep, the doctor got up and stood close to his sleeping friend. Chillingworth reached forward, pulled open the reverend's religious robes, and looked at Dimmesdale's chest. (Dimmesdale had always kept his chest covered. He never even let Chillingworth, his own doctor, examine him without his shirt on.) As soon as Chillingworth saw Dimmesdale's chest, a look of disbelief and excitement exploded on his face. He saw something that shocked and thrilled him, and he ran from the room. Once out in the hall, he leapt in the air and threw his arms gleefully over his head. If anyone could have seen this strange victory dance, they would have seen just how the Devil looks when he has won another soul.

CHAPTER ELEVEN

The Interior[1] of a Heart

Now that Chillingworth was sure that he knew Dimmesdale's secret, he tortured him at every opportunity. Whenever he could, Chillingworth would make comments or suggestions to make Dimmesdale fear that his secret had been revealed. Dimmesdale couldn't understand why Chillingworth was acting this way. As time went on, Dimmesdale began to fear—and even hate—his former friend.

Being a religious man, Dimmesdale began to feel guilty for hating his friend and physician. In

---

[1] **interior**—inside.

fact, Dimmesdale began to think that hating Chillingworth was his own sin. It was his fault, not Chillingworth's words, that made him hate the man.

With each passing day, Dimmesdale's health grew worse. Soon, everyone in the church was aware that Dimmesdale was becoming sicker and more nervous—he was thin, he had no energy, and he had no **appetite.**[2] Dimmesdale's own suffering made him more sympathetic to the problems of his church members. This made him better at giving advice to the people in his church and more under-standing of people's pain. His sermons were better than ever. All these changes in him made Dimmesdale more popular and more beloved by the people who went to his church.

The church members didn't know that all the good things in Dimmesdale were caused by his sin and guilt. In fact, the church members praised Dimmesdale even more. They said that God had given Dimmesdale his new-found sympathy, power, and wisdom because of his hard work and holiness.

Dimmesdale knew he was becoming more admired and that people were praising his hard

---

[2] **appetite**—a desire for food.

work. Dimmesdale knew he didn't deserve the praise—after all, he had sinned and kept his sin a secret. His guilt made him suffer even more, which made the members of his church love him all the more.

As things became worse, Dimmesdale reached the point where he knew that the only way he could get over his guilt, the only way he could clear his **conscience**,[3] was to confess. He needed to make his confession in public to be forgiven. But Dimmesdale couldn't bring himself to confess, even though it was the only way he could save himself. Dimmesdale tried to admit to his sins during his sermons, but he couldn't come right out and say what he had done. He made statements about his own weakness and sin, but he never mentioned adultery. No one in his church suspected that Dimmesdale was Pearl's father. Instead, the members of his church felt that Dimmesdale's confessions showed how holy he truly was.

Because Dimmesdale couldn't bring himself to admit that he had slept with Hester and that Pearl was his child, he began to punish himself for his sin. Late at night, when no one could hear, Dimmesdale locked himself in his room and

---

[3] **conscience**—sense of right and wrong; ideas and feelings inside of a person that warn of what is wrong.

whipped his back until it bled, laughing bitterly while he did it. Other times, he spent whole days without eating. Then he forced himself to go all night without sleep.

When he stayed awake all night, Dimmesdale's mind was filled with strange visions. He imagined seeing demons, angry angels, and his friends and parents, scowling with disgust and disappointment. Sometimes, he saw Hester and Pearl. Hester pointed at her scarlet letter, then at Dimmesdale's own chest.

On one of these ugly nights, Dimmesdale was struck with a new idea. Like a sleepwalker, he got up from his chair and began to dress in his most formal church robes. As he walked out the door, dressed for noon services (although it was the middle of the night), he thought to himself, "This might bring me a moment's peace of mind."

CHAPTER TWELVE

The Minister's Vigil[1]

Dressed in his finest religious clothes, Dimmesdale walked down the street as if in a dream. He stopped at the scaffold. Seven years before, Hester had stood here before the mob with Pearl. Dimmesdale was filled with shame. He could stand up there now, in the dark, where no one could see him. But seven years before he couldn't stand there with Hester and accept his guilt. He felt so ashamed that he cried out in the night. His painful cry caused many people, even the Governor, to look out their windows. But no one saw Dimmesdale on the scaffold.

---

[1] **vigil**—staying awake for some purpose; a night spent in prayer.

After a minute of **panic**,[2] Dimmesdale calmed down. As he stood on the platform, trying yet again to prepare his confession, he heard footsteps. Reverend Wilson was walking toward him. He had just come from the bedside of a dying man. Reverend Wilson was thinking about the man who had passed away just moments before, so he didn't even notice his friend on the scaffold. Dimmesdale tried to find the strength to call out his confession to Reverend Wilson. But he just let him pass by.

Dimmesdale stood alone on the platform for a long time. As the night got cold and damp, he began to wonder what would happen if his legs stiffened up and he couldn't get down. How odd it would be, for everyone to wake up and find him on the punishment platform, half frozen and fully dressed for church. Suddenly, Dimmesdale was struck by how funny this picture would be, and he began to laugh. He was even more shocked when a tiny, familiar laugh answered back.

Dimmesdale called out, "Who's out there?"

Hester and Pearl stepped up onto the platform. Pearl stood between Hester and Dimmesdale, holding their hands and linking herself and her two parents. The moment that Dimmesdale took Pearl's

---

[2] **panic**—a sudden fear or terror.

hand, he felt as if new life flowed through him. The three formed a chain—Dimmesdale felt new energy, even though lately he had felt sick and tired.

Hester and Dimmesdale didn't know what to say to each other. Only Pearl spoke.

She asked Dimmesdale, "Will you stand here with me and my mother tomorrow?" But Dimmesdale said he would not. Pearl tried to pull her hand away, but Dimmesdale held it tightly.

Again, Pearl asked, "Will you take my hand and my mother's hand tomorrow at noon?"

Dimmesdale answered, "Not then, but I will take your hand another time."

"When?" asked Pearl.

Dimmesdale told Pearl that they would all stand together there on Judgment Day.[3] As he spoke, a strange, red light filled the sky. Looking up, Dimmesdale thought he saw, in the black night sky, a huge glowing red *A*. Then the falling star burned itself out, and the night sky was dark again.

While Dimmesdale was staring at the flaming red A in the sky, he had felt Pearl pulling on his hand. He looked to see what Pearl was pointing at, and was stunned to see Roger Chillingworth standing in front of the platform. Dimmesdale

---

[3] Judgment Day—In some religions, a day of God's final judgment of the world; the day God decides who goes to Heaven and who goes to Hell.

looked down at the man and shivered when he saw Chillingworth's cold, cruel smile.

Turning to Hester, Dimmesdale said, "Hester, please, tell me who that man is. If he is a real person, and not some demon, tell me who he really is." But, remembering her promise to Chillingworth, Hester was silent.

"Dimmesdale," said Chillingworth, "you are too important a man in the community to act so foolishly. You must have been sleepwalking. Come down off there and follow me." So Dimmesdale followed Chillingworth away from the scaffold and into the night.

On the next morning, a Sunday, Dimmesdale gave one of the best sermons of his career. After the services, one of the townspeople came up to the reverend, holding one of Dimmesdale's gloves.

Dimmesdale's heart froze when the man said, "Here is your glove, Reverend. It was found on the punishment scaffold early this morning." Dimmesdale's mind began to spin, trying to dream up some excuse for his glove to have been on the platform.

Before he could answer, the man said, "I'll bet Satan stole it and left it there to mock your holiness."

As he was leaving, the man who had found the glove said, "Reverend Dimmesdale, sir, did you see the sign in the sky last night?" With this, Dimmesdale put his hand over his heart, feeling like he was going to faint.

"Reverend," said the man, with great seriousness, "I know what the red letter *A* in the sky stands for." Dimmesdale felt terrified, but also overjoyed. He felt that he had been discovered, and that the man would blurt out the truth and free him from his secret.

He felt that he had been discovered, and that the man would blurt out the truth and free him from his secret.

"It stood for *Angel*, Reverend. An important townsman passed away last night. The sign in the sky means that he was made an angel, don't you think?"

"I don't know," Dimmesdale said. "I don't have any idea what you are talking about. I heard nothing about a strange sign in the sky!"

CHAPTER THIRTEEN

Another View of Hester

After the meeting at the punishment platform, Hester made an appointment to meet with Dimmesdale to discuss their situation. In the light of day, she had a chance to look at Dimmesdale. She was shocked by how different he looked! It had only been seven years since Hester and Pearl stood before the crowd, but Dimmesdale looked much more than seven years older. He was pale, thin, and looked nervous and shaky. As she talked to him, she could tell that his mind was still strong, but his nerves and confidence were almost destroyed.

Of course, Hester had also changed over the seven years. When she first got out of prison, Hester didn't complain about her low position in society or the way the other people in town treated her. She found her place in society by cheerfully and tirelessly giving help to the sick, the poor, and the troubled. Her good attitude and helpfulness to others eventually won her the respect, even admiration, of the townspeople.

As time went on, in fact, the people's memory of her bad **reputation**[1] began to vanish. She had done so many good things for people, like caring for the sick, that some of the townspeople said that the letter *A* stood for *Able*, rather than *Adultery*. Many of the townspeople came to feel that Hester's letter was a **badge**,[2] a symbol of her hard, selfless work. The people in town became proud of Hester. People would say to each other, "There goes our Hester. She's so kind, so helpful, and so good."

Although Hester didn't think so, the people in town began to view the letter on her chest as a good luck charm or a special shield. It made Hester different from everyone else. Some said the letter had magical power to protect her from harm. There

---

[1] **reputation**—what people think and say of a person.

[2] **badge**—an emblem showing that someone has achieved something.

was even a story that an Indian's arrow had once struck the letter and bounced off.

But the hard years had changed Hester. She had been a bright, warm, and beautiful woman. Now she was cold—she hardly ever laughed or smiled. The warm glow had left her skin, and she hid her long, beautiful hair under a tight, white cap. Before, she would help others with an air of **dignity**[3] and **grace**.[4] Now, she acted like a **humble**[5] servant.

Hester felt alone in the world. Sometimes she worried about the responsibility of protecting and raising Pearl by herself. Although she loved the little girl, Pearl's odd behavior troubled her. She wondered if it was possible for anything good to come out of her shameful union with Dimmesdale.

There were times when Hester became so sad that she thought about killing herself and Pearl. The Puritans considered suicide evil. It was against God's law, so no one even dared to talk about it. Hester knew that thinking about killing herself was evil. To her, those "evil" thoughts were just more proof that the punishment of the scarlet letter was not enough to make her overcome her sins.

---

[3] **dignity**—proud character; self-respect.

[4] **grace**—goodwill; the favor and love of God.

[5] **humble**—not proud; low.

As she spent more time around Dimmesdale, Hester became more concerned about him. Would Dimmesdale become insane? She was also worried that it was her fault Dimmesdale was so sick. Dimmesdale was becoming weaker and weaker from being around Chillingworth. Hester wondered if it had been a mistake to keep Chillingworth's **identity**[6] a secret. As much as she wanted to save Dimmesdale by telling him who Chillingworth really was, she felt that she should keep this one promise to her husband.

Finally, she decided that she should at least talk with Chillingworth. Maybe he would release her from her promise. So Hester set out to look for Chillingworth. She wanted to talk with him about their secret. She found Chillingworth near the seashore, collecting **herbs**[7] for his medicines.

---

[6] **identity**—being one person and not another; in this case, identity means "who he is."

[7] **herbs**—plants used for medicine.

CHAPTER FOURTEEN

Hester and the Physician

Hester told Pearl to go play by the water. Pearl went down and looked at her reflection in the water and tried to talk her reflection into playing with her. Pearl wandered out into the shallow waters, while her mother went to talk with the man picking plants.

"I've heard a lot about you lately, Hester," said Chillingworth. "The townspeople are discussing whether it would be safe to the well-being of the town if your scarlet letter were removed. It appears that all of the kind things you have done have made a good impression. Of course, I told them that I thought it was a good idea."

"It's not up to them to take this letter off me," said Hester. "If I didn't deserve the letter, it would fall off."

"Wear it if you want," Chillingworth **sneered**.[1] "You've made it look beautiful, so wear it."

While they were talking, Hester stared at the old man. Seven years had added lines to his face, but he seemed to be strong and alert. He used to look calm, serious, and smart. Now he had a hard, cold, and evil look. He tried to cover up this look with smiles and friendliness. Even so, every once in a while, his true, dark nature would flash across his face. It occurred to Hester that after so many years of doing the Devil's work, Chillingworth had come to look like the Devil himself. Hester thought that Chillingworth's years of **tormenting**[2] Dimmesdale had succeeded in driving Dimmesdale crazy. It had also cost Chillingworth his soul.

Hester thought that Chillingworth's years of tormenting Dimmesdale had succeeded in driving Dimmesdale crazy. It had also cost Chillingworth his soul.

As they talked, Hester told Chillingworth that she was sorry she had ever agreed to keep his identity a secret. She should have told everyone who he really was. She was especially sorry because

---

[1] **sneered**—showed scorn or disrespect through words.

[2] **tormenting**—causing very great pain.

her silence had allowed Chillingworth to work his evil on Dimmesdale.

"I could have destroyed your lover and sent him to prison or the **gallows**.[3] So you had no choice. Don't feel guilty for your role in his doom," Chillingworth said. "Besides, I have done him no real harm. My excellent doctoring is the only thing that has kept him alive."

> "There is no good way for any of this to end, so at least let it end with the truth."

"It would have been better if he had died, rather than live a life of misery!" said Hester.

"Maybe it would have been better if he had died," Chillingworth agreed. "Then my hatred for him wouldn't have turned me into a demon."

"Haven't you done enough? Hasn't he paid you in full for what you think he did to you?" asked Hester.

"Paid me enough?" Chillingworth yelled. "Not even close! In fact, his debt is greater now than ever. He has further wronged me by turning me into this demon."

"Then it is as much my fault," Hester said. "I have also made you into a demon. Please forgive

---

[3] **gallows**—a wooden structure that is used for hanging criminals.

me for this. Release me from my promise to you. I must tell your secret so that Dimmesdale can know why you've tormented him. I don't know what will happen when I tell him, but he has suffered enough. Do whatever you want to him, but I want to tell him your secret. There is no good way for any of this to end, so at least let it end with the truth."

The doctor was moved by Hester's powerful words. "It's not up to me to forgive Dimmesdale . . . or you, Hester. I'll leave that up to God. We are all stuck in this terrible, unhappy mess, which began when you betrayed me with Dimmesdale. When I found out what you had done, I did what I had to do. Now go ahead—do what you want. Tell Dimmesdale who I am if you want to. I am done with him."

CHAPTER FIFTEEN

Hester and Pearl

Hester walked away from Chillingworth, but then turned back to look at him. He was a bent old man whose beard almost touched the ground when he leaned over.

Hester said softly to herself, "I know it is a sin to hate. But I hate that man." In Hester's mind, her own greatest crime was marrying Chillingworth, a man she did not and could not love. At least she had loved the man with whom she had committed her sin.

While the adults had talked, Pearl had played by the seashore. After Hester left Chillingworth, Pearl returned to her mother. Pearl had used seaweed to make a cap, a scarf, and a letter *A* for her shirt.

"Pearl," said Hester, "take off that *A*. It doesn't mean anything on you."

"Well, mother, what does it mean on you?" Pearl asked. Hester was surprised by the question and tried to ignore Pearl. But Pearl kept asking her mother about the *A*.

"Why do you wear the *A*, Mother? I know it has something to do with why the minister always keeps his hand over his heart."

At first, Hester smiled at Pearl's odd remark. But then she was shocked to realize that these two things did have a connection.

Meanwhile, Pearl would not stop asking, "Why do you wear the letter? Why does the minister keep his hand over his heart?"

Hester was tempted to tell Pearl the truth. Maybe then Pearl could finally understand their strange and lonely life. But Hester knew she couldn't tell Pearl the truth about what she and Dimmesdale had done.

Pearl wanted an answer, however, so Hester said, "Dear, I don't know anything about the minister's heart. I wear this letter every day because I like the gold stitching."

Of course, Pearl was not fooled by this answer. With a look of mischief, she continued to question her mother. Finally, when Pearl was still asking the next morning, Hester had to threaten to put Pearl in the closet if she didn't quit asking the same question over and over.

CHAPTER SIXTEEN

A Forest Walk

Now that she had permission to tell Chillingworth's secret, she couldn't wait to tell Dimmesdale. But Hester didn't want to go into Dimmesdale's apartment to tell him, so she kept trying to run into him around town. She found out that he was with a **missionary**[1] at a local Indian camp. Hester was so anxious to tell Dimmesdale the truth about Chillingworth that she and Pearl set off into the forest to find the minister.

As the two walked through the woods, Pearl played games trying to catch rays of light that were shining through the trees.

---

[1] **missionary**—someone who works to teach others religion.

"See, Momma," Pearl said. "I can catch the light, because I don't have the Black Man's mark on me. I'll bet you can't catch it."

Hester stretched her hands out to the light as she walked along, but she could never seem to catch the sun's rays in her hand.

"Pearl, I met the Black Man one time . . . and he did leave this mark on me."

"Pearl!" Hester said. "Who told you about the Black Man and his mark?"

Pearl said, "I heard an old woman in town say that there's an evil, dark man who lives in the woods here. She knows that he tries to get people to sign their names with their blood in the Black Man's book. Then he places his mark on the chests of those who sign. The old woman also told me that your red letter is the Black Man's mark."

Pearl continued to quiz Hester about the Black Man and his mark. Finally Hester said, "Pearl, I met the Black Man one time . . . and he did leave this mark on me."

The mother and child sat down by a **brook**,[2] deep in the forest. They sat silently, listening to the sad bubbling of the stream. Then, Pearl heard

---

[2] **brook**—stream.

footsteps—someone was coming. She cried out and ran to her mother, yelling, "Is it the Black Man? I want to see the Black Man!"

Then, from out of the bushes, came Reverend Dimmesdale, struggling to walk, with his hand clutched over his heart.

CHAPTER SEVENTEEN

The Pastor and His Parishioner

Dimmesdale walked slowly along the path and at first did not notice Hester.

She called out, "Arthur! Arthur Dimmesdale!" He thought that some forest spirit was calling him. He was relieved to see that it was Hester.

They moved into the shadow of the woods to talk. They both knew that it was time to talk about their past, but they began by chatting about the weather and other small talk. After a long silence, Dimmesdale looked deep into Hester's eyes.

"Have you finally found peace?" he asked. She looked down, sadly, at her letter and gave a weak smile.

"Have you?" she asked.

"No, none!" he answered. "I've had nothing but worry and sadness. I've been tormented so much. I feel like someone is always trying to find me out. The members of my church admire me, but I know what a terrible sinner I am!"

"Come now, good Reverend," Hester said. "I'm sure your love of God and your sorrow for your sin have been enough to remove the black mark from your name."

"I haven't been forgiven, because I haven't confessed."

He answered **bitterly**,[1] "No, no Hester. I haven't been forgiven, because I haven't confessed. You are so lucky to wear that letter on your chest. No one can see mine, but it is always burning inside me. I know I must confess, but there is no one in the world I can open up to. If I had one friend—or even an enemy—to tell my secret to, I would be **unburdened**.[2] This would set my soul free."

Hester leaned forward, full of pain at having to tell Dimmesdale this terrible secret. "Arthur, you have had such an enemy living with you, every day, all along. He lives under the same roof as you."

---

[1] **bitterly**—with pain and regret.
[2] **unburdened**—freed from a heavy load.

Upon finding out that Chillingworth was his enemy, that Chillingworth had been out to get him all along, Dimmesdale leapt to his feet, cried out, and clutched his heart with his hand.

"Please, please forgive me, Arthur. I wanted to tell you all along, but . . . Roger is my husband!"

"I can't believe you helped him torment me so long," Dimmesdale cried. He shook with anger, and Hester was afraid that he had finally lost his mind.

Hester reached for him. "Please forgive me, Arthur. If nothing else, I've always tried to be true. Truth is the one thing that I could hold on to. No one could take that away from me. I never wanted to hurt you, of all people. Please forgive me. The only reason I lied was that my husband swore he'd destroy you. He said he would tell everyone our secret if I told who he really was. Can you ever forgive me?"

"I do forgive you, Hester," Dimmesdale responded. "May God forgive us both! But there is someone who has sinned worse than we have. Chillingworth's revenge has been blacker than any sin. He broke a human heart. Hester, you and I never did that!"

As they talked, Dimmesdale's worst fears of the last seven years became real. He realized now that Chillingworth knew his secret. At any moment,

Chillingworth could destroy him. This thought completely discouraged Dimmesdale. It filled him with sadness, as if blackness had fallen over him. It seemed to Dimmesdale that his only escape would be death, but his Puritan beliefs were too strong. He knew he couldn't kill himself.

"Hester," he whispered, "you must help me. I don't know what to do. I need you to help me decide. I can't go back and live in the same house as Chillingworth! I'm afraid to be in the same town as he is. If he thinks that we might tell people who he really is, then he might tell everyone our secret! I should just lay down and die."

Hester began to cry, seeing how scared and pitiful Dimmesdale had become.

"Is this world so small! There are a million paths you can follow, all leading to a place where the dark shadow of Roger Chillingworth won't fall on you. Turn to the sea that brought you here. Let it take you away."

"I can't leave my job," Dimmesdale sighed. "To quit would mean disgrace and dishonor."

"But if you stay, and Roger tells our secret, or if he drives you mad, disgrace and dishonor wait here for you, too. Run away, Arthur. Create a new life in our old world of Europe. Do anything— preach, write, act . . . do anything but die!"

"Hester," Dimmesdale cried, "you are telling a man too weak to stand to run halfway around the earth. I don't have the strength or the courage to go out into the world alone."

"You won't go alone," whispered Hester.

CHAPTER EIGHTEEN

A Flood of Sunshine

Dimmesdale stared at Hester with a mixture of
disbelief[1] and joy. Her words frightened him—she
had said things that he could never have dared to
speak. Hester had been away from other people for
so long, treated like an outcast, that she was used to
thinking differently than other people. Suggesting
that they run away was not a strange idea to Hester.
But Dimmesdale had lived for all those years under
the laws of the church and society. It was hard for
him even to think about running away.

Dimmesdale was lost in thought. Then he
spoke, "If I had had one instant of peace or hope
in the last seven years, I'd stay here and hope for

---

[1] **disbelief**—not believing.

mercy.[2] But since I'm doomed here, there's no reason for me to stay."

"You are going," Hester said to him.

"Am I really feeling joy and hope again?" the minister wondered aloud. "I thought I could never be happy again. I threw myself down on this floor of leaves to die. Now I am rising up, born again."

"Let's not look back," Hester said. "The past is gone. Let's throw it away . . . like this!" And then Hester Prynne, the woman who had worn a symbol of her shame every day, tore the scarlet letter off her chest and threw it out into the woods.

"Now, it is gone—it's like it never existed."

With the letter gone, Hester felt free for the first time in seven years. She didn't realize how heavy the weight was until she didn't have it to carry anymore. She felt so free that she even took off the tight, dull, white cap, letting her long, full hair fly. She was filled with the energy of freedom and joy. She stood up, flung her arms open, and was suddenly bathed in a warm, bright ray of sun. The sunlight seemed to change her—she regained her spirit, her energy, and her beauty.

---

[2] **mercy**—kindness; being forgiven.

She grabbed Dimmesdale's hands and said, "And you have to get to know my Pearl . . . I mean, our Pearl. She is a strange child, but I know you'll love her, just like I do."

"But do you think she'll love me?" he asked. "I've never been good with children, and I've always been frightened by Pearl. She is so wild and mischievous!"

Pearl walked toward her parents, stepping from spots of sunshine into patches of shade. The animals of the forest weren't afraid of Pearl, and she seemed more at home there than in the town—she was calmer and happier. She approached her mother slowly. She was staring at the minister sitting next to her mother.

CHAPTER NINETEEN

The Child at the Brook-Side

"You will love her dearly," Hester repeated. "Look at how beautiful she is. She even has your eyes." Pearl was near now, and she stared at Dimmesdale with eyes that looked exactly like his own.

"You know, Hester," he said, "that I was always afraid of her little face. I was always afraid that one day, her face would look just like mine, and our secret would be discovered."

"Before long, you'll never have to fear anyone finding out that she is our child. Because we'll all be away from here and everyone then will know she is ours."

"You know children are afraid of me," Dimmesdale said. "No child has ever liked me. But wait—only twice has a child ever liked me. Twice, in her little lifetime, Pearl has been kind to me!"

Pearl had come close to her mother and father, but the little stream lay between them and the child. Pearl stood by a wide spot in the stream, where a strange, shimmering reflection of herself could be seen in the water. To Hester, it felt as if Pearl was a different person than the little girl she had always known. From the minute that Hester had taken off the *A*, her badge of shame, Pearl seemed different. Pearl had always been fascinated by the *A*. Hester had always thought of Pearl and the *A* together. Both the letter and her child were symbols of her sin, her pride, and her love. But she had thrown the *A* away, and now Pearl would not cross the stream to join her.

"Come here, Pearl," Hester called. "Come here, now, or I'll be angry with you!" But Pearl pointed at her mother's chest, and a frown darkened her small face. Pearl stamped her foot angrily, then threw herself on the ground and had a **tantrum**[1].

---

[1] **tantrum**—a fit of bad temper.

"I see now," said Hester. "She is upset because I look different: my letter is gone."

"Do whatever you need to do to make her calm down," said Dimmesdale. "She is making me nervous. It's like she is the spirit of the forest who haunts us, but can't cross the brook."

"Look, Pearl," Hester called, "the letter is right there at the edge of the brook. Bring it to me." Still, Pearl wouldn't budge.

"Bring it here, child!" Hester urged.

Pearl responded, "Come here, Mother. You pick it up."

"What has come over her?" asked Hester. "But she's right. I must wear this terrible symbol a few days more, until we leave this place. Then I can leave the scarlet letter behind me."

Hester picked up the letter and fastened it back on her chest. She tied up her hair and put back the tight cap covering her head. As she did so, she was **transformed**.[2] By putting her Puritan "costume" back on, she once again became the sad, dull, older-looking gray shadow of a woman—all the light and brightness were gone.

Hester looked up at Pearl. "Do you recognize me now? Will you finally come here?"

---

[2] **transformed**—completely changed.

"Now I will," Pearl said, leaping across the stream to hug her mother. "Now you are my mother, and I'm your little Pearl." Pearl gently kissed her mother. Then she gave the same loving kiss to the scarlet letter.

"Come now, and see the minister," Hester said. "He loves you, and he loves me, too. Come and love him, so we can all be together."

"Will he walk through the town with us," Pearl asked, "hand in hand for everyone to see?"

"Not today," said her mother, "but soon. Soon, the three of us will have our own life and our own home, and he will be your loving father."

"And will he always keep his hand over his heart?" Pearl asked.

"That's a silly question," Hester replied. "Now come and see the minister."

Pearl approached the minister, but she did not act friendly toward him. She seemed **jealous**[3] of him, as if she thought that the reverend would try to steal her mother away. Feeling nervous and awkward, Dimmesdale leaned forward and gave Pearl a kiss on the forehead. Immediately, Pearl ran to the stream and splashed her forehead with water, trying to wash the kiss away.

---

[3] **jealous**—being afraid that someone you love may love someone else.

CHAPTER TWENTY

The Minister
in a Maze

Dimmesdale left the forest before Hester and Pearl.
Walking back to town, he thought about his
and Hester's secret plan. They had decided that
Europe would provide a new life for them. The
weather would be better for Dimmesdale's health,
and Pearl would be able to go to good schools. A
ship bound for Bristol, England, was to set sail in
four days. Hester had met the captain before. She
was going secretly to buy tickets for two adults and
one child to England.

Dimmesdale was very interested in the exact
time the ship would leave. When Hester told him

it was going to leave in four days, Dimmesdale was excited.

"The timing is perfect!" he said. The reverend was supposed to give the Election Day sermon (a highlight in any minister's career) on the day before the ship left. He wanted to finish all his duties before he left.

The excitement and relief Dimmesdale felt caused him to have more energy than he had had in many years. He almost flew as he hurried along the path to his home. He felt so changed that he wanted to greet people he passed in the street and yell, "I'm not who you think I am! I left him back in the forest." He ran into one of the older men of his church, and he was overwhelmed with the urge to start babbling and shouting **blasphemies**.[1]

As Dimmesdale passed through town, more **bizarre**[2] thoughts filled his head.

"What's my problem?" he wondered. "Have I gone mad? Has the Devil fully gained control of my soul?" As he was thinking this, Mistress Hibbins (the woman who would later be tried as a witch) stepped before him.

---

[1] **blasphemies**—words that show contempt for God or sacred things.

[2] **bizarre**—very odd or fantastic.

As if reading his mind, she said, "So, you have made a visit to the forest? Next time, let me know, and I'll go with you to meet the Black Man. He is my friend, and I can put in a good word for you."

Had an evil spirit come for him? Yes, one had—and its name was Roger Chillingworth.

"Madam," the minister declared, "I have been to the woods, but not to seek the Devil. In fact, I was meeting with a missionary who was bringing God to the Indians."

"Oh, of course," **cackled**[3] the witch. "We must pretend not to be Devil-worshipers when we are out in public. I'll see you at midnight in the forest, brother."

This caused the minister to wonder about his and Hester's bold plan. Maybe he had been tricked by the Devil. Was that why he had been filled with such strange and immoral thoughts since leaving the forest? Had the Devil tempted him with a dream of happiness? He was relieved when he reached his apartment and was able to go inside.

His relief was broken by a knock on the door. Had an evil spirit come for him? Yes, one had—and its name was Roger Chillingworth. The minister

---

[3] **cackled**—laughed in a harsh way.

was now fully aware of the doctor's evil intentions toward him. And the doctor sensed that the reverend no longer regarded him as a trusted friend, but as an enemy. Each knew the other's secret, but neither one spoke of the ill will between them. Instead, they exchanged small talk, then they retired to their separate rooms.

CHAPTER TWENTY-ONE

The New England Holiday

Three days after Hester and Dimmesdale's meeting in the forest, it was Election Day. The governor who had just been elected was going to take office, and Dimmesdale was going to give the sermon. Hester and Pearl came to town to see the events. Although she was filled with joy on the inside, Hester wore her usual gray clothes. She also wore her letter *A* as if to say, "Take a last look at the letter and the person who wears it. Soon she'll be gone, and you'll never have her to look down on again."

Pearl, dressed colorfully as usual, asked her mother why the town was so full of strangers.

Why was everyone in town taking time away from work? Hester explained that the parade to celebrate the new governor would be passing by. The day was a holiday for everyone, and all the town would be there.

"Oh good, Mother. Then will the minister come stand with us and hold our hands, in front of everyone?"

"He'll be here, Pearl," Hester said. "But he won't speak to you, and you can't speak to him, today."

"What a strange, sad man he is," Pearl said. "He calls us to see him in the nighttime, but he won't speak to us during the day. And he always covers up his heart with his hand."

"Be quiet, Pearl. These are things that you are too young to understand," Hester said.

The crowd was filled with all kinds of people. Frontiersmen, Indians, somber **clergymen,**[1] townsfolk, serious Puritans, excited children, rough wild-looking men who worked on the sea . . . and Roger Chillingworth, talking quietly with the captain of the ship on which Hester and Dimmesdale planned to escape.

---

[1] **clergymen**—ministers or pastors.

The captain walked over to Hester. Although the crowd was shoulder-to-shoulder thick, there was a lonely circle of space around Hester.

"Well, Ms. Prynne, I'll have to have my ship **steward**[2] make room for one more passenger. But we have no fear of illness on this voyage, with my ship's doctor and this other doctor."

"What other doctor?" Hester gasped.

"I'm sure you knew Dr. Chillingworth planned on traveling with us," the captain replied. "You must have known, because he says he is an old friend of yours and is traveling with you. He tells me that he's a close friend of the gentleman you are traveling with, the one who is having problems with these strict old Puritan rulers."

"They know each other well, indeed," Hester mumbled. "They have lived together for a long time." An ocean of sadness fell upon her. She looked up then, across the square, and saw the hard, dark face of old Roger Chillingworth. He smiled at her . . . a smile that carried with it a secret and fearful meaning.

---

[2] **steward**—person who works on a ship and looks after the passengers.

CHAPTER TWENTY-TWO

The Procession[1]

Before Hester could decide what to do about this terrible turn of events, she heard the music of the oncoming parade. She and Pearl watched the procession with interest, and so did all the other townspeople. When Reverend Dimmesdale came by, all the people were struck by his energy and high spirits.

Hester looked at the energetic, confident man who marched toward her. She could hardly believe this was Dimmesdale. He seemed nothing like the sad, frightened man in the forest. Yes, he was

[1] **procession**—something that moves forward in an orderly way, like a parade.

different. Would he give her a secret **glance**?[2] Maybe the meeting in the woods had never happened—maybe there was no love or plan to escape between them!

"Mother!" said Pearl. "Is that the same minister from the forest, the one who kissed me? I wouldn't know him! He looks so different."

"Yes, child," Hester said. "But hush. We can't speak in public of the things that happen to us in the forest."

"If I had known it was he," Pearl said, "I would have run up to him, grabbed his hand, and asked him to kiss me in front of everyone. What would he have done then?"

"It's good that you didn't do this," Hester said. "This is not the place, or the time, for kissing."

The old witch Hibbins stood next to Hester. "Look at him," Hibbins said. "Who would know that he was the sinner that met with you in the forest? Don't try to **deny**[3] it. I've spent enough time in the forest that I can recognize the others who have spent time there in the Devil's company. And another thing I know is that when someone pretends not to be a sinner, to not know the Devil, the Black Man places a mark on him for all to see.

---

[2] **glance**—a quick look.

[3] **deny**—say that something is not true.

I wonder what Reverend Dimmesdale is hiding, when he always keeps his hand over his heart."

Hester and Pearl edged close to the platform, where Dimmesdale was now beginning to speak. The sermon was the most powerful he had ever given. The whole audience felt the wisdom and beauty of his words. While Hester listened, Pearl ran around the square and played. Everyone enjoyed watching the bright, colorfully-dressed child as she played among the crowd. The ship's captain pulled her aside.

> *"I wonder what Reverend Dimmesdale is hiding, when he always keeps his hand over his heart."*

"Please take a message to your mother," the captain told Pearl. "Tell her that Dr. Chillingworth said he'll bring your mother's friend to my ship. She only needs to get herself and you there. Give her this message, little witch baby."

Pearl's face turned dark and serious. "Mistress Hibbins says my father is the dark prince of the underworld. If you call me 'witch' again, I'll have my father chase you and wreck your ship!"

Pearl passed the message on, and the bad news was almost enough to destroy all of Hester's hope. Hester was also bothered by another problem. Today there were many people from out of town who had come to see the procession. They had heard of, but never seen, the famous scarlet letter Hester wore. Knowing that she was near to the time that she could throw the letter into the sea forever, Hester could hardly stand the stares of these strangers. The letter burned into her chest worse than it had before. And while they all stared at Hester, no one would stand near her.

While Hester stood apart in her shame, Dimmesdale stood up on the scaffold, a holy, respected man. He was adored by the crowd. Even in their wildest imaginations, the people couldn't have dreamed that both Hester and Dimmesdale were marked with the same sign of shame!

CHAPTER TWENTY-THREE

The Revelation[1] of the Scarlet Letter

When Dimmesdale's voice finally fell silent, the crowd began to speak. Everywhere, people were turning to each other to talk about the greatest sermon that anyone had ever heard. Dimmesdale was having at that moment the single greatest success of his whole life. Never before had he been so popular, so well-respected, so powerful. The crowd cheered for their minister. All the while, Hester stood next to the platform with the red letter burning on her chest.

---

[1] **revelation**—making something known.

Then, Dimmesdale walked shakily toward Hester and Pearl. The energy he had shown during his sermon was gone. He appeared drained and pale. He turned toward Hester and Pearl and opened up his arms.

"Come here, Hester. Come here, my little Pearl," he said. Pearl flew to him, wrapping her arms around his legs. Hester came up to him much more slowly. At the same time, Chillingworth came out from the crowd and walked toward Hester, Pearl, and Dimmesdale.

"You're too late, tempter," Dimmesdale said firmly. "With God's help, I'm going to escape from you now."

Chillingworth grabbed Dimmesdale by the shoulder. "Ignore them, friend. Tell them to go away. Don't destroy your reputation. I can still save you!"

"You're too late, tempter," Dimmesdale said firmly. "With God's help, I'm going to escape from you now."

He opened his arms and held Hester and Pearl close to him.

"Hester Prynne, in the name of the all-powerful God who gives me life and strength to do what I must do now, I held myself back seven years ago.

I can't do it again. Share your strength with me, for it is God's will for us to be together. This bitter old man will try to stop us. Come, support me! Stand up here on the scaffold with me!"

Hester and Reverend Dimmesdale, with Pearl holding Dimmesdale's hand, climbed the scaffold together. The crowd was in shock. The church and city leaders were so shocked by the confession that they all stood, frozen, like statues. Chillingworth followed the newly formed family onto the platform.

Chillingworth glared at the reverend. "There is nowhere in the whole world where you could have escaped me, no secret place in the world where you could hide, except here in front of everyone, up on this scaffold."

"Thanks be to God, then, who led me up here!" Dimmesdale cried out. "Hester, isn't this even better than we dreamed in the forest?"

"I don't know," Hester said. "What will happen to us now? Will you, Pearl, and I die?"

"For you and Pearl, your life will be whatever God decides," Dimmesdale answered. "I am a dying man; so now, before it's too late, I'll take your shame away from you and put it onto me!"

Supported by Hester, Dimmesdale turned slowly to face all the stunned leaders and people of Boston.

"People of New England, who have loved me and thought me a holy man. I am here, where I should have stood seven years ago with this woman and our child. You have all stared at Hester and her letter *A*, but there is one of us whose mark of shame you've never shuddered at. But God and all his angels saw it. The Devil knew of the mark as well. The man who wore the mark cleverly hid it, so that none of you could see it. It burned my flesh every moment. Behold before you a sinner!"

Then, Dimmesdale tore open his shirt, and everyone gasped in shock and horror at what they saw on his chest.

Then, Dimmesdale tore open his shirt, and everyone gasped in shock and horror at what they saw on his chest. He stood, while the crowd stared at their minister. Finally, he **collapsed**.[2]

Chillingworth knelt over Dimmesdale, but the doctor's face was dull and blank.

"You have escaped me, Dimmesdale. Curse you, you have escaped me for good!"

---

[2] **collapsed**—broke down; fell to the ground.

Dimmesdale responded, "May God forgive you, because you, too, have sinned deeply."

Dimmesdale called weakly to Hester and Pearl. "Pearl, will you kiss me now? You wouldn't before. Will you now?" Pearl kissed his lips, and her tears fell on her father's face. It was as if a spell had been broken. As the child cried over her father, her strangeness and wildness seemed to fall away from her.

"Hester, farewell," said the dying man.

Hester asked, "Will we meet again? Will we be together forever in the afterlife?"

"Hester," Dimmesdale whispered, "remember our sin. God is forgiving, but we sinned against him when we violated our respect for God and for our souls. I doubt we'll share eternal happiness together, but God has proved his mercy by what he's done to me. He gave me this mark, He sent that dark and evil man to keep the mark painful and red hot, and He's brought me here to die as an example to the people that I love. If God hadn't sent any of these punishments to me, my soul would have been lost forever. Praise God, His will be done."

And Dimmesdale's last word was "Farewell."

CHAPTER TWENTY-FOUR

Conclusion

After a few days passed, when people had a chance to calm down, several stories were told of what happened that day. Most people swore that they saw a red letter *A* on Dimmesdale's chest, **imprinted**[1] on his flesh. Some people said that Dimmesdale had burned it on himself. Others said that Chillingworth had caused it by his medicines, or that it was a sore that had made its way out of Dimmesdale's heart and onto his chest. The reader can decide what to believe about where the mark came from.

There were some people who claim to have seen the whole thing and saw no letter on

---

[1] **imprinted**—marked deeply and permanently.

Dimmesdale's chest. Those people also denied that he confessed to being Pearl's father. According to these witnesses, he died in Hester's arms to serve as a holy example of forgiveness. Most people think that this version of the story was created by Dimmesdale's friends and supporters, who wanted to see the minister's good reputation live on.

Maybe the lesson to be learned from Dimmesdale's miserable experience is "Be true to yourself. Show the world what you really are, and admit to what you have done."

It should also be noted that as soon as Dimmesdale died, an incredible change came over Chillingworth. He lost his energy and his power, and he appeared small and shriveled. He died within the year. Without his hate and his mission to destroy Dimmesdale, he had nothing left to live for. In the old man's will, he left most of his **estate**[2] to Pearl. This is how Pearl became the richest **heiress**[3] in the New World. The demon's daughter (as some townspeople had always thought of her) gained a new status and respect in the town. She probably

---

[2] **estate**—a person's property and possessions that are divided up when a person dies.

[3] **heiress**—a woman who inherits great wealth. (To inherit is to receive someone's property and possessions after the person dies.)

would even have married into a fine, Puritan family and become a leader of the community. I say "would have," because, not too long after Chillingworth's death, Hester and Pearl vanished. For many years, rumors of Hester and Pearl came from across the sea, but no one knew for sure what had become of the two.

And when she turned, the children could see a flash of color, a scarlet letter on her chest!

The legend of the letter remained strong for many years, and people treated the scaffold in the marketplace and Hester's abandoned cottage as cursed, haunted places.

Then one day many years later, a group of children saw a tall, older woman in a gray robe go up to the empty cottage. She opened the door, ready to enter. But then she turned away from the door for an instant, as if unwilling to return to the place of her former, unhappy life. And when she turned, the children could see a flash of color, a scarlet letter on her chest!

Hester had returned, but she returned without Pearl and lived completely alone. No one ever found out what became of Pearl, although Hester received letters, gifts, and expensive **trinkets**[4] from overseas. Whoever sent these things to Hester obviously possessed great wealth. The only other clue about what happened to Pearl was that Hester was once seen embroidering a beautiful outfit for a baby.

People were amazed to see that Hester had taken up her burden, her scarlet letter, again. She had a chance to be free of it, and to never see the town where she was humiliated and abused again. Yet she had come back of her own free will.

As time went on, Hester became a respected and important part of the community. There was a steady parade of villagers to the lonesome cottage, especially women, who came to her for comfort when they were troubled. Hester maintained her plain, quiet humbleness, because she believed that no one marked by sin should be proud or should feel special.

Many years later, a grave was dug for Hester, near the older grave of Reverend Dimmesdale. A space was left between Dimmesdale's and Hester's graves, as if they would never be side by side, even

---

[4] **trinkets**—small ornaments, such as rings and jewels.

in death. But one tombstone bore both their names, together at last. At the top of that tombstone you can still see today a **crest**[5] with faded words beneath it. The crest and words tell this whole tale very simply, but very few understand the meaning of the faded letters, which read:

"On a black shield, the letter *A*, in red."

---

[5] **crest**—a decoration, usually used by a particular family or group.